OLD-TIME COWBOY SONGS

For
Anneliese Cannon

Revised Edition
15 14 13 12 11   5 4 3 2 1

Published by
Gibbs Smith
P.O. Box 667
Layton, Utah 84041

1.800.835.4993 orders
www.gibbs-smith.com

Designed by J. Scott Knudsen
Cover designed by Kurt Wahlner
Printed and bound in Korea

Gibbs Smith books are printed on either recycled, 100% post-consumer
waste, FSC-certified papers or on paper produced from sustainable PEFC-
certified forest/controlled wood source. Learn more at www.pefc.org.

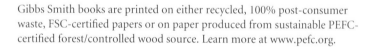

The Library of Congress has cataloged the earlier edition as follows:

Old-time cowboy songs.

   Melodies with guitar chords; each song precede by the words printed as text.
   Bibliography: p.
   1. Folk music—West (U.S.) 2. Folk-songs, English—West (U.S.)
3. Ballads, English—West (U.S.) 4. Cowboys—West (U.S.)—Songs
and music. 5. Cowboys—West (U.S.)—Poetry. 6. Cowboys—West
(U.S.)—Songs and music—Texts. 1. Cannon, Hal, 1948–
M1629.6.W504   1988   87-754169
ISBN: 0-87905-308-9 (first edition)

ISBN: 978-1-4236-2061-7 (revised edition)

OLD-TIME COWBOY SONGS

Edited by Hal Cannon

GIBBS SMITH
TO ENRICH AND INSPIRE HUMANKIND

Contents

★Songs are on the tape recording

Introduction

To many westerners, any country music played at taverns is cowboy music. In contrast, to working cowboys and ranch people, cowboy songs are those whose stories tell of the occupation of riding horses and raising cattle.

It used to be that cowboy and western music were synonymous in the minds of most Americans. But there are differences: country music is based on traditions of the rural Southeast. A new western traditionalism in music has been growing which resents the "western" being taken out of country and western. Working cowboys (and cowgirls) take seriously the mythic qualities of their lives. They still dress like cowboys, stake a good percentage of their earnings on fancy saddles and hand-crafted gear, many recite poems and sing cowboy songs. They risk all to cultivate the immense amount of skill it takes to be a good hand, taking seriously values such as valor, gentlemanliness, and honest work in the open lands of the West.

People of the West came to this part of the country from all over the world. They brought their old traditions with them, adapting and keeping some, discarding others. Just as western settlement was at its peak, means of communication in the world changed dramatically; telephones, phonographs, film, and radio brought popular culture to a new height of importance in people's lives.

Westerners needed some basis for identity in a rapidly changing technological world. Simultaneously, Americans became fascinated with cowboys. A handful of artists, writers, folklorists, and poets began to record the music, craft, and work skills. Recording artists of western songs in the twenties were primarily working cowboys who sang the folk music of their occupation. Often these boys put a simple melody to any old cowboy poem, making a song. (Many of those narrative songs are better suited for recitation, but a couple with good melodies are included here.)

As western movies became popular, many of their songs were composed in New York, performed in four-part harmony and fully orchestrated—a far cry from the cowboy folk music which preceded. The best of this new music, however, still responded to the heartfelt romance for cowboy lifestyle, and was therefore claimed by westerners. Over the last half century the power of popular culture is unmistakable. In some sense, applying the technologies of popular culture to folk expression is like putting a jet engine in a model T Ford. With the cowboy song, sometimes the wheels flew off the old fliver, but sometimes the supercharged cowboy song with overtones of jazz and pop styling worked quite nicely and was embraced by the folks of the West.

Many cowboys and western music enthusiasts are now looking back to early recordings made by working cowboys and western musicians to find a sense of tradition which responds to the unique land, sky, climate, and settlement of the West. Thanks to a few pioneering folklorists there is a good record of the text of cowboy music, and regional record companies captured the spirit of early cowboy singers. Many of the selections in this book were composed between 1880 and 1930. Even for the most familiar of them, I have chosen old and often archaic versions.

The songs herein were picked as favorites by a loose group of musicians called the Bunkhouse Orchestra, or the Deseret String Band. Most of the tunes are simple—sparse like the desert—so for decades they have been overlooked for their musical value; yet, just about every song in this volume has a melody that will cling to you like a bur.

This is a simple, sturdy little song book which was made to be used. Take it out in the wilds, like any field guide, where the singing of old western songs can be accompanied by the sputter of a campfire or the soft percussion of wind through the aspen leaves.

Acknowledgments

Nearly twenty years ago a group of jolly adventurers made regular trips to the wild desert lands of southern Utah. As children of technology, we had discovered the beauties of dashboard cassette players in our vehicles. While searching for music which worked with the landscape we found some old cowboy recordings from the twenties and thirties. Our first and most prominent influence was an L.P. album of Victor reissues—old 78s edited by Fred Hoeptner. Though now unavailable, the music on that record is uniformly stunning. After getting hooked on this record and other reissues of old-time music we began ordering cassettes from collectors of 78s. We listened and learned the music. The leaders in this informal cassette sharing scheme were Greg Schaub and Tom Carter, to whom I am indebted. The artistic forces behind gathering this music—learning to love it, sing it, and appreciate the cowboy way—came to us from singers credited before each song. I personally must thank present and past members of the Deseret String Band: Leonard Coulson, Mark Jardine, Stephen Jardine, Rich McClure, Skip Gorman, Tom Carter, and Ron Kane. I also have a debt of gratitude to musicians, cowboys, and others who give these songs meaning: Gibbs Smith, Mark Rassmussen, Bertram Levy, Waddie Mitchell, Rand Hillman, Doug Green, Ian Tyson, Jim Griffith, Mike Korn, Mike Seeger and the New Lost City Ramblers.

Annie Laurie
William Douglas and Lady John Scott

Cowboys sing not only songs about cowboy life but popular songs of the day. Here is a well-known Scottish song, followed by a poem about its effects on a broken-hearted cowpoke. The poem I learned from a recitation by Owen Johnson, Moccasin, Arizona.

Maxwelton's braes are bonnie, where early falls the dew,
And twas there that Annie Laurie gave me her promise
    true;
Gave me her promise true, which ne'er forgot will be,
And for bonnie Annie Laurie, I'd lay me down and die.

Her brow is like the snowdrift, her throat is like the swan;
Her face it is the fairest, that e'er the sun shone on;
That e'er the sun shone on; and dark blue is her eye,
And for bonnie Annie Laurie, I'd lay me down and die.

A Bad Half Hour
Charles Badger Clark

Wonder why I feel so restless;
Moon is shinin' still and bright,
Cattle all is restin' easy,
But I just kain't sleep tonight.
Ain't no cactus in my blankets,
Don't know why they feel so hard—
'Less it's Warblin' Jim a-singin'
"Annie Laurie" out on guard.

"Annie Laurie"—wish he'd quit it!
Couldn't sleep now if I tried.
Makes the night seem big and lonesome,
And my throat feels sore inside.
How *my* Annie used to sing it!
And it sounded good and gay
Nights I drove her home from dances
When the east was turnin' gray.

Yes, "her brow was like the snowdrift"
And her eyes like quiet streams,
"And her face"—I still kin see it
Much too frequent in my dreams;
And her hand was soft and trembly
That night underneath the tree,
When I couldn't help but tell her
She was "all the world to me."

But her folks said I was "shif'less,"
"Wild," "unsettled,"—they was right,
For I leaned to punchin' cattle
And I'm at it still tonight.
And she married young Doc Wilkins—
Oh my Lord! but that was hard!
Wish that fool would quit his singin'
"Annie Laurie" out on guard!

Oh, I just kain't stand it thinkin'
Of the things that happened then.
Good old times, and all a-past me!
Never seem to come again—
My turn? Sure. I'll come a-runnin'.
Warm me up some coffee, pard—
But I'll stop that Jim from singin'
"Annie Laurie" out on guard.

Back To The Range

This song was originally recorded by one of the great tight- harmony singing brother duos of this half century, the Delmore Brothers.

Ten years ago I left my home to be a city slicker;
Take me back (take me back) to the range.
Once more the plains I long to roam and hear my
  bronco knicker;
Take me back (take me back) to the range.

Refrain:

Take me back to the range and the campfire;
Let the night wind blow over me;
At the set of sun when work is done and coyotes start to
  prowl,
Then let them whine, take me back to the range.

When the white stars gleam, then let me dream, a-way
  out on the prairie;
Take me back (take me back) to the range.
In the rain or snow I'll always go, I'll never be contrary;
Take me back (take me back) to the range.

Refrain

Oh, Pinto Pete, I long to greet, he was my old-time
  buddy;
Take me back (take me back) to the range.
Side by side we used to ride when the trail was mighty
  muddy;
Take me back (take me back) to the range.

Refrain

There's a little girl I left behind when I first started
  roamin';
Take me back (take me back) to the range.

She said that she would sure be mine, I guess I'll soon be
    goin';
Take me back (take me back) to the range.

Blue Mountain

Fred Keller

Fred Keller spent his younger days as a cowboy in the country around Monticello, Utah. He wrote this song to preserve his memories after he left the cowboy life to move to town. He ended up as a well-loved judge in Price, Utah, where he lived until the late 1970s.

My home it was in Texas,
My past you must not know;
I seek a refuge from the law
Where the sage and piñon grow.

Refrain:

Blue Mountain, you're azure deep,
Blue Mountain with sides so steep,
Blue Mountain with horse head on your side,
You have won my heart for to keep.

I chum with Latigo Gordon,
I drink at the Blue Goose saloon,
I dance at night with the Mormon girls,
And I ride home beneath the moon.

I shop at Mons' store
With bullet holes in the door;
His calico treasure my horse will measure
When I'm drunk and feeling sore.

In the summer the wind doth whine,
In the winter the sun doth shine
But say there, brother, if you need a mother,
There's Ev on the old chuck line.

The Boaster (Gay Paree)

This interminable song was learned from Effie Carmack of Kentucky. Originally written for the Tin Pan Alley circuit by McGlennon, Conley, and Sayers in 1893, no one can sing it like Leonard Coulson.

I've been in gay Paree
Where the wind at half past three
Came strolling along where the boys belong
Hollering "Ta Ra Boom de Aye."

I've danced the oyster can
Upon the American plan
And I've shed great tears when I got three years
For stealing a couple of Texas steers.

I've been in Kansas C,
I've been out on a spree,
I've been in jail, been out on bail
And I've been on a ship that would not sail.

I've been in Ohio, likewise in Buffalo,
Indianapolis, Cincinnati, Louisville and Cameo,
I've been up in a balloon, been in a saloon,
I've been dead broke and I've been in soak
And I've drank and drank 'til I thought I would croak.

I've been an awful dude,
And sometimes rather rude,
I've had hard luck and I've been dead stuck
And I've been the driver of a two-horse truck.

I've been in many a scrap,
I've had a real hard slap,
My eyes have been draped in mourning and crepe
For a year and a half I've been stuck on my shape.

I've been in bum hotels,
Paid prices that were swells,

Slept in bum beds and dying and bled
Chasing bedbugs round my head.

Been buncoed once or twice
With cards and shaking dice,
Bet a house and a lot and a fourteen spot,
And they pulled my leg plumb full of knots.

I've often played baseball,
Been umpire and all,
Been hit with clubs and sticks and bricks
And floundered about in a terrible fix.

And I've been in Chicago too,
That place where the wind blew through.
And I went to the fair where they clipped my hair,
Charged me a dollar an inch for air.

And I went down on the track,
At a race horse took a crack,
Bet a ten or two on a horse I knew,
But the horse dropped dead and he never came to.

I've lived on pork and beans,
Oh, I've slept in room thirteen,
Been out at night and I've seen the sights,
And I've hit the pike by candlelight.

I've been in Salt Lake too,
'Twas the only place I knew,
Where the girls were beauties and they did their duties
And they chewed the gum called Tootsie Fruitsie.

I've been in Ind-i-an
and stepped on a ba-nan,
I slipped, I fell, it hurt like hell,
But the words I used I must not tell.

I also rode a wheel,
Run an automobile,
I've had a prize fight and I had a gold strike,
Since that night I've never been right.

A fought for the Blue and the Gray,
I've slept on a bale of hay,
Drove a mule, taught public school,
But I never could find the golden rule.

I've drank red lemonade
That was made by a post hole spade,
And I've shot snipes by electric lights,
And I've marched with the Salvation Army at night.

I've been in politics too,
Oh, how the money flew,
At Tammany Hall I had a close call,
But I never could learn to sing "After the Ball."

I've been where I didn't belong,
You've heard this lovely song,
Now these are all facts but I made a few cracks,
And I got it in the neck where the chicken got the axe.

The Bravest Cowboy

Some of the best cowboy songs were recorded by southern musicians in the 1930s and '40s. This one we learned from the legendary North Carolina fiddler, Tommy Jarrell.

I am the bravest cowboy
that ever roamed the West.
I been all over the Rockies,
I got bullets in my breast.

In eighteen hundred and sixty-three
I joined the immigrant band.
We marched from San Antonio
Down by the Rio Grande.
When I was on the prairie
I learned to toe the line,
I learned to pocket money,
But I did not dress much fine.

When I was on the prairie
I learned to rob and steal, and
When I robbed that cowboy
How happy I did feel.

I wore a broad-brimmed white hat
And my saddle too was fine,
And when I'd court them pretty girls
You bet I called 'em mine.

I courted her for beauty,
But for love it was in vain,
'Cuz they carried me down to Dallas
To wear the ball and chain.

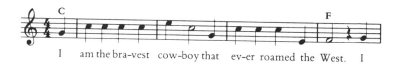

I am the bra-vest cow-boy that ev-er roamed the West. I

been all o-ver the Rock-ies, I got bul-lets in my breast.

The Brazos

This old Texas song came my way through Slim Critchlow. Ian Tyson also does a whale of a job with it.

We crossed the wide Pecos, we forded the Nueces,
We swum the Guadelupe, we followed the Brazos.
Red River runs rusty, the Wichita runs clear,
But it was down by the Brazos I courted my dear.

Refrain:

Li–le–li–lee, give me your hand, (repeat three times)
There's many a river that waters the land.

The fair Angelina runs glossy and gliding,
The crooked Colorado runs weaving and winding,
The slow Antonio courses the plain,
But I never will walk by the Brazos again.
Refrain 2:
Li–le–li–lee, Pull the boat on (repeat 3 times)
My Brazos River sweetheart has left me and gone.

She kissed me, she hugged me, she called me her
dandy.
The Trinity is muddy, the Brazos quick sandy.
She kissed me, she hugged me, she called me her own,
But down by the Brazos she left me alone.
Refrain

The girls of Little River they're plump and they're
pretty,
The Sabine and Sober have many a beauty.
By the banks of the Nacogdoches there's girls by the
score,
But down by the Brazos I'll wander no more.
Refrain

The Bunkhouse Orchestra
Badger Clark

This passel of words is supposed to go to the tune of "Turkey in the Straw." This isn't a song for everyone. It takes a certain talent to spit it out straight.

Wrangle up your mouth-harps, drag your banjo out,
Tune your old guitarra till she twangs right stout,
For the snow is on the mountains and the wind is on the
    plain,
But we'll cut the chimney's moanin' with a livelier
    refrain.

Shinin' 'dobe fireplace, shadows on the wall—
(See old Shorty's friv'lous toes a-twitchin' at the call:)
It's the best damn high that there is within the law
When seven jolly punchers tackle "Turkey in the
        Straw."

Freezy was the day's ride, lengthy was the trail,
Ev'ry steer was haughty with a high arched tail,
But we held 'em and we shoved 'em, for our longin'
    hearts were tried
By a yearnin' for tobacker and our dear fireside.

Swing 'er into stop-time, don't you let 'er droop!
(You're about as tuneful as a coyote with the croup!)
Ay, the cold wind bit when we drifted down the draw,
But we drifted on to comfort and to "Turkey in the
        Straw."

Snarlin' when the rain whipped, cussin' at the ford—
Ev'ry mile of twenty was a long discord,
But the night is brimmin' music and its glory is
    complete
When the eye is razzle-dazzled by the flip o' Shorty's
    feet!

Snappy for the dance, now till she up and shoots!
(Don't he beat the devil's wife for jiggin' in 'is boots?)
Shorty got throwed high and we laughed till he was
    raw,
But tonight he's done forgot it prancin' "Turkey in the
    Straw."

Rainy dark or firelight, bacon rind or pie,
Livin' is a luxury that don't come high;
Oh, be happy and unruly while our years and luck
    allow,
For we all must die or marry less than forty years from
    now!

Lively on the last turn! lope 'er to the death!
(Reddy's soul is willin' but he's gettin' short o' breath.)
Ay, the storm wind sings and old trouble sucks his paw
When we have an hour of firelight set to "Turkey in the
    Straw."

Bury Me Not On The Lone Prairie

This sad old ballad about the boy who can't stand the idea
of spending eternity buried in the western wilderness
comes in many different versions. It was probably first written as a sea burial by Reverend E. H. Chapin in 1839.

Oh, bury me not on the lone prairie
Where the coyotes wail and the wind blows free;
When I die don't bury me
'Neath the western skies, on the lone prairie.

"Oh, bury me not on the lone prairie,"
These words came soft and painfully
From the pallid lips of a boy who lay
On his dying bed, at the break of day.

But we buried him there on the lone prairie,
Where the rattlesnakes hiss and the wind blows free,
In a shallow grave, no one to grieve.
'Neath the western sky, on the lone prairie.

The Cowboy And The Lady

Before the rake from New Mexico stepped into this song, a sailor had occupied the place of the seductor in these verses for a hundred or two hundred years. Jim Griffith from Tucson learned this ditty from I. D. Jones of San Simon, Arizona, and passed it on to me.

One morning, one morning, one morning in May
I spied a fair couple who went on their way,
And one was a maiden and fair for to see
And the other a cowboy, a bold feller was he.

Good morning, good morning, good morning cried
    they.
And where are you going this beautiful day?
We're going, we're going to the banks of Cold Springs
To see the waters rushing, hear the nightingale sing.

So onward together this couple did go
Till they came to a place where the clear waters flow.
He sat down beside her by the banks of Cold Springs
To see the waters rushing, hear the nightingale sing.

They had not been gone for an hour or two
When out from his budget a fiddle he drew.
He played her a tune, caused the valleys to ring,
Hark, hark, cried the maiden, hear the nightingale sing.

Oh ho, said the cowboy, it's time to give o'er,
Oh no, cried the maiden, just play one tune more.
So he played her a tune, caused the valleys to ring,
Hark, hark, cried the lady, hear the nightingale sing.

Oh ho, cried the maiden, won't you marry me?
Oh no, said the cowboy, that never could be.
I've a wife in New Mexico and children twice three,
Two wives on a cow ranch, too many for me.

I'll go back to New Mexico, I'll stay there one year,
Instead of cold water, I'll drink wine and good beer.
And when I return 'twill be late in the spring,
To see the waters rushing, hear the nightingale sing.

The Cowboy's Dance Song
James Barton Adams

This is another old poem which has been set to music, often abbreviating the song with fewer verses. Glenn Ohrlin sings this one well.

Now you can't expect a cowboy to agitate his shanks
In the etiquettish fashion of aristocratic ranks,
When he's always been accustomed to shake the heel
    and toe
In the rattling ranchers' dances where much etiquette
    don't go.
You can bet I set there laughing in quite an excited way,
A giving of the squinters and astonished sort of play,
When I happened into Denver and was asked to take a
    prance
In the smooth and easy measures of a high-toned dance.

When I got among the ladies in their frocks of fleecy
    white,
And the dudes togged out in wrappings that was simply
    out of sight,
Tell you what, I was embarrassed and somehow I
    couldn't keep
From feeling like a burro in a purty flock of sheep.
Every step I took was awkward and I blushed a flaming
    red,
Like the upper decorations of a turkey gobbler's head.
And the ladies said 'twas seldom they had ever had a
    chance
To see an old-time puncher at a high-toned dance.

I cut me out a heifer from that bunch of purty girls,
And I yanked her to the center to dance those dreamy
    whirls.

She laid her head upon my breast in a loving sort of way
And we drifted into heaven while the band began to
    play.
I could feel my neck a burning from her nose's
    breathing heat
As she docey-doed around me, half the time upon my
    feet.
She looked up into my blinkers with a soul-dissolving
    glance
Quite conducive to the pleasures of a high-toned dance.

Every nerve just got to dancing to the music of delight,
And I hugged that little sagehen uncomfortably tight;
But she never made a beller and the glances of her eyes
Seemed to thank me for the pleasures of a genuine
    surprise.
She cuddled up against me in a loving sort of way,
Tell you what, the joys of heaven ain't a cussed
    circumstance
To the huggamania pleasures of a high-toned dance.

When they struck the old cotillion on that music bill of
fare,
Every bit of devil in me seemed to bust out on a tear;
I fetched a cowboy war whoop and I started in to rag
Till the rafters started sinking and the floor began to
sag.
My partner she got sea sick, and then she staggered for a
seat,
And I balanced to the next one but she dodged me slick
and neat.
Tell you what, I took the creases from my
go-to-meeting pants
When I put the cowboy trimmings on that high-toned
dance.

Now you can't ex-pect a cow-boy _ to a-gi-tate his shanks, In the

e - ti-quet-tish fash-ion of a - ris-to-cra-tic ranks, _ When he's

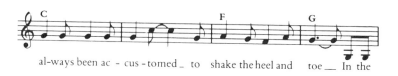

al-ways been ac - cus -tomed _ to shake the heel and toe __ In the

rat-tling ran-chers' dan-ces where much e - ti-quette don't go.

Cowboy Jack

Of all the cowboy songs I have collected in Utah, this sentimental one seems to be sung by more of the old-timers than any other, at least in our country. This is Glenn Ohrlin's version of the song.

He was just a lonely cowboy
With a heart so brave and true,
And he learned to love a maiden
With eyes of heaven's own blue.

They learned to love each other
And named their wedding day.
But a quarrel came between them
And Jack he rode away.

He joined a band of cowboys
And tried to forget her name.
But on the lonely prairie
She waits for him the same.

One night when work was finished,
Just at the close of day,
Someone said, "Sing a song, Jack,
Will drive dull care away."

When Jack began his singing
His mind did wander back,
For he sang of a maiden
who waited for her Jack.

Refrain:
Your sweetheart waits for you, Jack,
Your sweetheart waits for you
Out on the lonely prairie,
Where the skies are always blue.

He left the camp next morning,
Breathing his sweetheart's name.
"I'll go and ask forgiveness,
For I know that I'm to blame."

But when he reached the prairie
He found a new-made mound.
His friends they sadly told him
They'd laid his loved one down.

They said as she was dying
She breathed her sweetheart's name
And asked them with her last breath
To tell him when he came.
Refrain

He was just a lone-ly cow-boy

With a heart so brave __ and __ true,

And he learned to love a __ maid-en

With eyes of __ heav-en's own blue.

A Cowboy's Life

While the song is sung in a lot of different versions, this one talks of "Chinaman's charms." I believe this comes from a time when Chinese style and having Chinese domestic help was popular in cultivated circles in the West, thus contrasting the gentleman's life with the hard life of a cowboy. Heard first by Sloan Mathews of Alpine, Texas. Leonard Coulson assembled several versions into this one.

Refrain (before each verse):
Talk about your farms and your Chinaman's charms,
Talk about your silver and your gold.
A cowboy's life is a very dreary life,
It's a-riding thru the heat and the cold.

Early every morning you'll hear the boss say,
"Get up, boys, it's the breaking of the day,
It's now for to rise with your sleepy little eyes
And your bright dreamy night's passed away."

When springtime comes double hardship has begun,
The rain is so fresh and so cold,
We almost freeze from the water on our clothes
And the cattle you can scarcely hold.

A cowboy's life is a very dreary life,
Some say that it's free from all care,
Rounding up the cattle from the morning till the night,
In the middle of the prairie so bare.

The wolves and the owls, with their terrifying howls,
Disturb us in our midnight dream,
While we're lying in our slickers on a cold and rainy
    night,
Way over on the Pecos stream.

I used to roam around, but now I stay at home,
Cowpunchers take my advice:
Sell your saddle and your bridle,
Quit your roving and your travel
And marry you a pretty little wife.

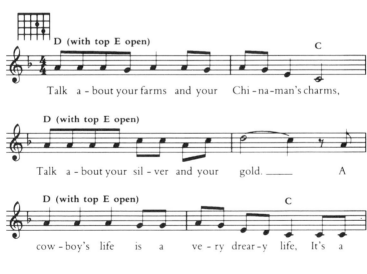

The Cowboy's Soliloquy
Allen McCanless

Not only does this preach a most accurate sermon about
cowboy spirituality, it has an equally alluring melody to
match the words. I learned it from a 1924 recording of Carl
Sprague.

All day o'er the prairie alone I ride,
Not even a dog to run by my side;
My fire I kindle with chips gathered round,
And boil my coffee without being ground.

Bread lacking leaven' I bake in a pot,
And sleep on the ground for want of a cot;
I wash in a puddle and wipe on a sack,
And carry my wardrobe all on my back.

My ceiling the sky, my carpet the grass,
My music the lowing of herds as they pass;
My books are the brooks, my sermons the stones,
My parson's a wolf on a pulpit of bones.

But then if my cooking ain't very complete,
Hygienists can't blame me for living to eat;
And where is the man who sleeps more profound
Than the cowboy who stretches himself on the ground.

My books teach me constancy ever to prize,
My sermons that small things I should not despise;
And my parson's remarks from his pulpit of bone,
Is that "the Lord favors those who look out for their
　　own."

Between love and me lies a gulf very wide,
And a luckier fellow may call her his bride;
But Cupid is always a friend to the bold,
And the best of his arrows are pointed with gold.

Custer's Last Charge

This song is an adaptation of a Civil War song which ends the same way—message: no one wins in war. A couple of different Utah versions were combined to come up with this one.

It was just before brave Custer's charge
Two soldiers drew their reins,
With parting words and clasping hands
They might never meet again.
One was a tall and a slendery lad,
And had trusted all in the one
That he loved best, so well, in hand,
She was all this world to him.

"Upon my breast I have a face,
I'll wear it in a fight;
A face that is all this world to me
It shines like a morning light.
Like a morning light was her love to me
For she cherished a lovely smile,
And little have I cared for another face
Since she promised to be my wife.

"Will you write to her, Charlie, when I am gone,
Send back that fair fond face,
And tell her gently how I died
And where is my resting place?"
Tears filled the eyes of the blue-eyed boy
And his sad heart filled with pain.
"I'll do your bidding, brave comrade mine,
If we never do meet again.

"But if I get killed will you ride back
And do as much for me?
I have a mother who's waiting at home

And she's all this world to me.
One by one she lost us all,
She lost both husband and son,
And I was the last that our country called
And she kissed me and sent me on.''

Just then the order came to charge,
With an instant clasp of hands,
An on and on and on they rode,
This brave and devoted band.
They returned from the hill that they could not gain
Where the Indians shot like hail
And poured out death on Custer's ranks
And scalped them as they fell.

Among the dead who were left behind
Was a boy with curly hair,
And the cold dark form that rode by his side
Lay dead beside him there.
No one was left to tell the blue-eyed girl
The last words her lover had said,
And the aged mother who's waiting at home
Will learn that her boy is dead.

It was just be - fore brave Cus - ter's charge Two
sol - diers drew __ their reins, With __ par - ting
words and clasp - ing hands They might ne - ver
meet __ a - gain. One was a tall and a
slen - de - ry lad, And had trust - ed all in the
one That he loved best, so well in
hand, She was all this world __ to him.

The Days Of Forty-Nine
Charley Rhodes

Aperson could research all the meanings of these
antiquated words but nearly a hundred and fifty years
later this song still provides only a colorful impression of the
days of the California gold rush. Charley Rhodes, a
banjoist-minstrelist, penned this number. I learned it through
George Taggart of Salt Lake City.

You see before you old Tom Moore,
A relic of bygone days.
The people call me Bummer Shore.
But what care I for praise?
O when I think of the days that's passed,
It makes me grieve and pine
For the days of old and the days of gold,
And the days of forty-nine.

There's New York Jake, the butcher boy,
So fond of getting tight.
Whenever Jake got on a spree
He was spoiling for a fight.
One night he ran against a knife
In the hands of old Bob Kline,
And over Jake we held a wake
In the days of forty-nine.

There was Poker Bill, one of the boys
Who was always in for a game.
He'd deal for you and he'd deal for me;
To him it was all the same.
He'd ante a slug or force the jack,
He'd bet a hatful blind.
In a game with death Bill lost his breath
In the days of forty-nine.

There's old lame Jess, a tough old cuss,
Who never would repent;
He never was known to miss a meal
Or ever throw in a cent.
But poor old Jess like all the rest
To death he did resign,
And in his boom went up the flume
In the days of forty-nine.

Of all the comrades I had then
There's none left but me,
And all that I am waiting for
Is a senator to be.
The people cry as I go by,
"There goes the traveling sign,"
Crying, "Old Tom Moore
from Bummer Shore
In the days of forty-nine."

37

Dryland Farmers

Ilearned this telling little song about the encroachment of civilization from the late Kenneth Ward Atwood of West Jordon, Utah.

How well I do remember, how well I do recall
How we used to round them up, and brand them one and all.
Right on that same old spot where we used to rope the steers,
They're growing big potatoes and them little roasting ears.

Refrain:

Then we'll ride no more fat horses, and we'll have to sell our twine,
Go and eat that old sow bosom cut so damn close to the rind.

I rode up on a pinnacle and pulled off my slouch hat,
Then all that I could see was the farm shacks on the flat.
Said the Indian to the cowboy, "You'd better look around,
For you're liable to be camping on some other fellow's ground."

Now the Indians and the cowboys, they used to live in peace,
Till the damned old dryland farmers come a-creeping from the East.
Then we'll ride no more fat horses, and we'll have to sell our twine,
Go and eat that old sow bosom cut so damn close to the rind.

The Dying Ranger

These somber old cowboy songs were never sung more beautifully than by the Cartwright Brothers, and I don't mean Hoss, Little Joe, or what's-his-name. This song has been popular with cowboys since the 1830s.

The sun was sinking in the west, it fell with lingering
  rays
Through the branches of the forest where a wounded
  ranger lay
'Neath the shade of a palmetto and the sunset's silvery
  sky.
Far from his home in Texas, they laid him down to die.

Draw closer to me comrades, and listen what I say,
I'm going to tell a story, while the spirit hastes away
Way back in northwest Texas, that good old Lone Star
  State,
There's one that for my coming with a weary heart will
  wait.

A fair young girl, my sister, my only joy and pride,
I brought her up from childhood, I never left her side;
For our father lies a sleeping beneath the church yard
  sod,
And our mother too is sleeping in the bosom of her
  god.

I'm dying, comrades, dying, I must leave her all alone,
Who will be to her a brother, who will take her to his
home?
Up spoke the noble Rangers, they answered one and all,
"We will keep her as a brother, till the last one of us
falls."

A sad sweet smile of pleasure, o'er his pain-wracked
face did spread,
Then a dark and dusky shadow and the Ranger boy was
dead.
Far from his darling sister, we laid him down to rest,
With his saddle for a pillow, and his gun across his
chest.

The Gol Darned Wheel

There is something downright poetic when a seasoned old puncher applies his knowledge of horsemanship to the riding of one of those big-wheeled bicycles. This song was sung by Buck Lee on a 1946 recording by folklorists Austin and Alta Fife.

I can rope and ride the wildest bronco in the wild and
    woolly West,
I can rope and I can ride him, let him do his level best,
I can handle any critter ever wore a coat of hair,
But I had a lively tussle with a 'normous grizzly bear.

I can rope and tie the wildest longhorn in the the wildest
    Texas land,
And in any disagreement I can play a winning hand.
But at last I met my master and I surely had to squeal.
When the boys got me straddle of the gol darned wheel.

It was at the Eagle Rancho, on the Brazos as a jest
Ran across the damn contrivance that upset me in the
    dust.
Naturally up and throwed me, stood me on my cursed
    head,
Put my face in lightning order, as the foreman said.

It's a tenderfoot that brought it, he come wheelin' all
    the way,
From the sunshine end of freedom, by the San Francisco
    Bay.
He tied up at the Ranch, to get on the outside of a meal,
Never thinkin' that I'd monkey with his gol darned
    wheel.

Arizona Jim begun it when he said to Jack McGill,
That's a puncher broke the record riding on his braggin'
    skill.

Said as how there was a puncher not a million miles
away,
He thought his self a rider and he's terribly gay.

Such a slur upon my talents made me madder than a
mink,
And I told 'em I could ride it for amusement or for
chink.
For it's nothing but a plaything for the kids and such
about,
And they'd have their ideas shattered when they
trucked the critter out.

Well the grade was kinda sloping from the rancho to the
creek,
And we went a-gallaloppin' like a crazy lightnin' streak,
With a-whizzin' and a-buzzin' first to one side and to
that
The contrivance kinda wobbled like the flyin' of a bat.

And the boys began to holler, "Stay with him Uncle
Bill,
Shove the steel in the critter turn his muzzle up the hill."
Well I never said a word and I didn't look around,
Kept my two eyes busy lookin' for the smoothest
ground.

No I never said a word, and neither did I squeal,
I was building a reputation on the god darned wheel.
I held a sneaking idea as on down the hill I went,
That I ordered me a mix-up I couldn't circumvent.

Then the ground flew up and hit me and the stars all
tangled up,
And the last that I remembered was the punchers picked
me up.

They packed me to the Rancho and they stretched me
on the bed,
Cowboys gathered round me cause they knowed that I
was dead.
Jesus Christ and all his prophets how we split the Texas
air,
And the wind it made a popup of my sable skinny hair
How we met the Texas eagles and tore up the Texas
sod.
I cussed all that was holy and I also cussed my god.

And a doctor he was sewing on the skin where it was
ripped.
And old Arizona whispered, "Well, old boy I guessed
you're whipped."
And I told him I was busted from sombrero down to
heel,
And he grinned and said, "You ought to see that gol
darned wheel."

I can rope and ride the wild - est bron - co in the

wild and wool - ly West, I can rope and I can

ride him, let him do his le - vel best, I can

han - dle a - ny crit - ter e - ver wore a coat of hair, But I

had a live - ly tus - sle with a 'nor - mous grizz - ly bear.

LAMBERT

Golden Slippers

If you were going to pick the top ten dance hits of nineteenth-century western settlers who traveled in wagon trains, you would have to include this old minstrel song right up there with "Turkey in the Straw," "Buffalo Gals," and "The Gal I Left Behind Me."

Oh, the old banjo hanging on de wall
'Cause it ain't been a–tuned since a–way last fall,
Well I'll pull it down and we'll play a tune
When we ride the chariot in the morning time.

Refrain:

Oh dem Golden Slippers, oh dem Golden Slippers,
Dem Golden Slippers I'm gwine to wear 'cause dey
    look so neat;
Oh dem Golden Slippers, oh dem Golden Slippers,
Dem Golden Slippers I'm gwine to wear 'cross de
    golden street.

Oh we'll go downtown and we'll buy some shirts
And we'll buy some pants and we'll buy some shoes,
And we'll get right home and we'll be at home
When we'll try them on in the morning time.

    Refrain

Oh, the old ban - jo hang-in' on de wall 'Cause it
ain't been a-tuned since a - way last fall, Well I'll
pull it down and we'll play a tune When we
ride the char - iot in the morn - ing time.

Refrain
Oh dem Gol - den Slip - pers, Oh dem
Gol - den Slip-pers, Dem Gol - den Slip-pers I'm
gwine to wear 'cause dey look so neat;
Oh dem Gold - en Slip - pers, Oh dem
Gold - en Slip - pers, Dem Gold=en Slip - pers
I'm gwine to wear 'cross de gol - den street.

Herding Sheep For Granville Pace
Lot Alexander

T his true song about the hypocritical Mormon sheep
rancher has been kept alive by the author's niece, Della
Turner, of Washington, Utah.

On the fourteenth of October, I went a wild–goose
    chase,
From Washington to Harmony, to work for Granville
    Pace.
The evening I arrived there, he counted out my sheep;
I built my bed 'neath an old sage bush, but could not
    rest or sleep.

Refrain:

Dough gobs and boiled flank and castlebloat for tea,
An old sheep pelt and a ragged old quilt was all he'd
    furnish me!
A frying pan with the handle gone, and no pot to cook
    maize,
That's all in this world you'll ever get if you work for
    Granville Pace.

Now the first day that I herded, there came an awful
    fog;
I, of course, fell short some sheep, I did not have a dog.
When we got to the counting pen, Gran says, "You're
    out two sheep!"
Granville swore and Granville cursed, but he did not
    find the sheep.

Now he sent me out a damned old dog, and said her
    name was Nell;

The first time I set her on the sheep, she scattered them to hell!
I up with my rifle and took a shot at her; Granville never said a word, but he thought "You dirty cur!"

Refrain

On a Sunday we started for the desert, a-storming like hell,
Granville, he got homesick and said he wasn't well;
He went up to Pinto, and got in a heck of a fight,
Came sneaking back to the old sheep camp in the middle of the night.

Now when we got our new camp built, Gran often come around;
It was then Christmas time, of course we went to town;
We went up to Granville's to get a little "mon";
While we were a-sitting there, in the ward teachers come;
Granville says, "I pray each night, before I go to sleep."
But he forgot to tell of the time, when he stole Joe Prince's sheep!

Refrain

On the four-teenth of Oc-to-ber, I went a wild-goose chase, From Wash-ing-ton to Har-mo-ny to work for Gran-ville Pace. The eve-ning I ar-rived there, he coun-ted out my sheep; I built my bed 'neath an old sage bush, but could not rest nor sleep. Dough gobs and boiled flank and cas-tle-bloat for tea, An old sheep pelt and a rag-ged old quilt was all he'd fur-nish me! A fry-ing pan with the han-dle gone, and no pot to cook maize, That's all in this world you'll e-ver get if you work for Gran-ville Pace.

Hittin' The Trail Tonight
Bruce Kiskaddon

Bruce Kiskaddon is my favorite cowboy poet. He wrote a
few that seemed like they could take a melody. I made up
a tune and started singing it. It's a good one to break up an
evening get-together.

The moon rides high in the cloudless sky
And the stars are shinin' bright
The dark pines show on the hills below
The mountains capped with white.
My spurs they ring and the song I sing
Is set to my horse's stride
We gallop along to an old-time song
As out on the trail we ride.

Refrain:

I'm hittin' the trail tonite
I'm hittin' the trail tonite
My horse is pullin' the bridle reins
I'm hittin' the trail tonite.

You can hear the sound as he strikes the ground
On the frozen trail below
His hoof beats hit and he fights the bit
He's slingin' his head to go.
We'll ride the trail till the stars turn pale
And camp at the break of dawn,
Nobody will know which way I go,
They'll only know I'm gone.

I did not try to say goodbye,
Let somebody else do that,
I'll ride alone and I'll find a home
Wherever I hang my hat.

Let people that set and talk explain
Jest whether I'm wrong or right
My horse is pullin' the bridle reins
I'm hittin the trail tonite.

Second Refrain:

The moon shines down on the rollin' plains
And the tops of the mountains white
My horse is pullin' the bridle reins
I'm hittin' the trail tonite.
First refrain

Home On The Range

So what's a cowboy song book without this one? It was Franklin Roosevelt's favorite song. About a hundred people have claimed authorship, but it looks like it was first penned in 1873 by a saddle-bag physician from Indiana, Brewster Higby.

Oh give me a home where the buffalo roam,
Where the deer and the antelope play,
Where seldom is heard a discouraging word
And the skies are not cloudy all day.

Refrain:

Home, home on the range,
Where the deer and the antelope play,
Where seldom is heard a discouraging word
And the skies are not cloudy all day.

Where the air is so pure, the zephyrs so free,
The breezes so balmy and light,
That I would not exchange my home on the range
For all of the cities so bright.

The red man was pressed from this part of the West,
He's likely no more to return,
To the banks of Red River where seldom if ever
Their flickering campfires burn.

How often at night when the heavens are bright
With the light from the glittering stars,
Have I stood here amazed and asked as I gazed
If their glory exceeds that of ours.

Oh, give me a land where the bright diamond sand
Flows leisurely down the stream;
Where the graceful white swan goes gliding along
Like a maid in a heavenly dream.

Then I would not exchange my home on the range,
Where the deer and the antelope play;
Where seldom is heard a discouraging word
And the skies are not cloudy all day.

Refrain

I'd Like To Be In Texas For The Roundup In The Spring

This song is beautifully sung by Slim Critchlow and comes in a couple of good versions. This one seems to pull the heartstrings best.

In a lobby of a big hotel in New York town one day,
Sat a bunch of fellows telling yarns to pass the time
away.
They told of places where they'd been, different sights
they'd seen,
Some of them praised Chicago town and others New
Orleans.

In a corner in an old armchair sat a man whose hair was
grey;
He had listened to them eagerly to what they had to say.
They asked him where he'd like to be, his clear old
voice did ring,
"I'd like to be in Texas for the roundup in the spring."

Refrain:
I can see the cattle grazin' o'er the hills of early morn,
I can see the campfire smokin' at the breakin' of the
dawn,
I hear the coyotes yellin', I hear the cowboys sing.
Oh, I'd like to be in Texas for the roundup in the
spring.

They all sat still and listened to each word he had to say;
They knew the old man sittin' there had once been
young and gay.
They asked him for a story of his life out on the plain;
He slowly then removed his hat and quietly began.

"I've seen 'em stampede o'er the hills till you think
    they'd never stop,
And I've watched them run for miles and miles until
    their leaders drop;
I was foreman on a cow ranch, that's the calling of a
    king.
And I like to be in Texas for the roundup in the spring.

Refrain

There's a grave in sunny Texas where Molly Denning
    sleeps,
And a grove of mossy live oaks that constant vigil
    keeps.
In my heart's a recollection of that long long bygone
    day
When we rode the range together like truant kids at
    play.

Her gentle spirit calls me in watches of the night,
And I hear her laughter freshening the dew of early
    light.
I was the foreman of a cow ranch, that's the calling of a
    king.
I'd like to be in Texas for the roundup in the spring.

Refrain

In a lob - by of a big ho - tel in
New York town one day, Sat a bunch of fel - lows
tell - in' yarns to pass the time a - way. They
told of pla - ces where they'd been, dif - ferent sites they'd
seen, Some of them praised Chi - ca - go town and
oth - ers New Or - leans. *Refrain* I can see the cat - tle
graz - in' o'er the hills of ear - ly morn, I can
see the camp-fire smoke-in' at the break - in' of the
dawn, I hear the coy - otes yell - in', I
hear the cow - boys sing. I'd like to be in
Tex - as for the round - up in the spring.

Little Joe, The Wrangler

This song symbolizes old-time cowboy life to many cowboys I have met. Although it was never a commercial success, it has remained one of the best songs for insiders of cowboy culture. It was written by the first great cowboy song collector and banjo-toting-puncher, Jack Thorpe.

Little Joe, the wrangler, will never wrangle more;
His days with the "Remuda"—they are done.
'Twas a year ago last April he joined the outfit here,
A little "Texas Stray" and all alone.

'Twas 'long late in the evening he rode up to the herd
On a little old brown pony he called Chaw;
With his brogan shoes and overalls a harder looking kid
You never in your life had seen before.

His saddle 'twas a southern kack built many years ago,
An O. K. spur on one foot idly hung,
While his "hot roll" in a cotton sack was loosely tied
    behind
And a canteen from the saddle horn he'd slung.

He said he'd had to leave his home, his daddy'd married
    twice
And his new ma beat him every day or two;
So he saddled up old Chaw one night and "Lit a shuck"
    this way
Thought he'd try and paddle now his own canoe.

Said he'd try and do the best he could if we'd only give
    him work
Though he didn't know "straight up" about a cow,
So the boss he cut him out a mount and kinder put him
    on
For he sorter liked the little stray somehow.

Taught him how to herd the horses and to learn to
    know them all
To round 'em up by daylight; if he could
To follow the chuck wagon and to always hitch the
    team
And help the "cosinero" rustle wood.

We'd driven to red river and the weather had been fine;
We were camped down on the south side in a bend
When a norther commenced blowing and we doubled
    up our guards
For it took all hands to hold the cattle then.

Little Joe, the wrangler, was called out with the rest
And scarcely had the kid got to the herd
When the cattle they stampeded; like a hail storm, long
    they flew
And all of us were riding for the lead.

'Tween the streaks of lightning we could see a horse far
    out ahead
'Twas little Joe, the wrangler, in the lead;
He was riding "old Blue Rocket" with his slicker 'bove
    his head
Trying to check the leaders in their speed.

At last we got them milling and kinder quieted down
And the extra guard back to the camp did go
But one of them was missin' and we all knew at a glance
'Twas our little Texas stray, poor wrangler Joe.

Next morning just at sunup we found where Rocket fell
Down in a washout twenty feet below
Beneath his horse mashed to a pulp his horse had rung
    the knell
For our little Texas stray—poor wrangler Joe.

C   **F**

Lit‑tle Joe, the wrang‑ler, will ne‑ver wran‑gle

C

more; His days with the "Re‑mu‑da" they are

G   **C**

done. _____ 'Twas a year a‑go last

F   **C**

A‑pril he joined the out‑fit here, A

G   **C**

lit‑tle "Tex‑as Stray" and all a‑lone.

'Longside Of The Santa Fe Trail

I t's hard to think of this song without thinking of the droll
style of Glenn Ohrlin, though it came to me through old
recordings of Jules Verne Allen.

Say, pard, have you sighted a schooner
Way out on the Santa Fe Trail?
They made it here Monday or sooner
With a water keg tied on the tail.
There was Daddy and Ma on the mule seat
And somewheres along by the way
Was a tow-headed gal on a pinto
A-janglin'for old Santa Fe.

*Refrain (each refrain sing last line of verse after Yo ho):*Yo
    ho, a-janglin' for old Santa Fe.

I seen her ride down the arroyo
Way back on the Arkansas sand,
With a smile like an acre of sunflowers
And a little brown quirt in her hand.
She mounted her pinto so airy,
And rode like she carried the mail,
And her eyes near set fire to the prairie
'Longside of the Santa Fe Trail.

Oh, I know a gal down by the border
That I ride to El Paso to sight,
I'm acquainted with a high flying order
And I sometimes kiss some gals goodnight;
But, lord, they're all fluffles and beading
And afternoon tea by the pail,
Compared to the sort of stampeding
That I got on the Santa Fe Trail.

I don't know her name on the prairie;
When you're huntin' one gal in some ways
It's shorter from hell to helalee

Than it is on the Santa Fe ride.
But I'll maybe make Plumbers by sundown,
Where a camp may be made in the swale,
And I'll come on a gal with a pinto
Camped 'longside the Santa Fe Trail.

Maid Of Argenta
Jimmy Driftwood

Ron Kane learned this song when he was ten years old from a ten-inch disc of songs by Jimmy Driftwood, of "Battle of New Orleans" and "Tennessee Stud" fame, and taught it to me. I've never met any cowboys who knew this one.

As I was a-riding on the streets of Argenta,
I spied a fair maiden all dressed in magenta;
The riders who knew her all called her pimenta;
She was a beautiful dame.

I sprang from my saddle and I walked up beside her,
Said, "Where can we get some corn whiskey and cider?"
We walked down the street to a place called the spider
Where she turned my heart into flame.

I tried to be calm but my heart was so frisky,
I knew I was playing the game that was risky;
I looked in her eyes and could not drink my whiskey,
For she was an angel to me.

I cried, "Oh my beautiful maid of Argenta,
All dressed in the splendor of royal magenta,
If you will but promise to be my pimenta,
My heart yours forever shall be."

I gave her my gold and I gave her my cattle;
We both made a vow as we sat in my saddle;
Then I rode away the wild outlaws to battle,
And left her in old Arkansas.

When I returned home to my rock on the river,
I found she was gone and it made my heart quiver;
I cannot forget and I cannot forgive her,
And I can't get her out of my craw.

Now I sit alone in that place called the Spider,
Where I fell in love as I sat there beside her;
And all the day long I drink whiskey and cider,
And talk to all manners of men.

I tell them if ever I see the pimenta,
All dressed in the splendor of royal magenta,
I'd hug her right there on the streets of Argenta,
And we'd start all over again.

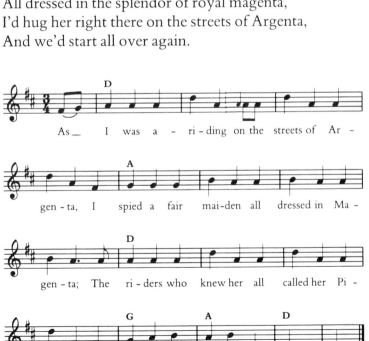

Mormon Cowboy

Through an early recording by Carl Sprague I learned this song. He learned it from friends near Globe, Arizona. This song is still sung there sometimes with the boy going home to safe innocence and other times marrying the wild and woolly girl met at the dance.

I am a Mormon cowboy, Utah is my home,
Tucson, Arizona, is the first place I did roam,
And then into El Capitan, a place you all know well,
To describe that brushy country, no mortal tongue can
  tell.

I was at the old post office, when a maid come riding
  down,
She rode a bronco pony and was soon upon the ground;
She gave to each and every man an invitation grand,
She invited us to a grand ball at the old El Capitan.

So we all went to the dance that night at the
  schoolhouse by the road;
Many folks come from Dripping Springs and many
  come from Globe;
The music they brought with them I never shall forget,
'Twas a colored man with his guitar; I can hear him
  playing yet.

There were many married women there and single gals
  too,
I soon became acquainted with all except a few;
The cowboys in their high–heeled boots were leading
  the grand march,
While the city dudes soon followed with their collars
  stiff with starch.

After dancing two or three sets I went outside to cool,

But every bush that I passed by was loaded with white
mule;
They finally fed us supper; it was a quarter past one;
I heard a fight had broken out, each cowboy pulled his
gun.

There was this little cow puncher, his eyes were flashing
fire;
He said he was the ramrod at a ranch called Bar F Bar.
I started for my pony; the guns were flashing fast;
Then I heard the cowboys shouting out, "We broke it
up at last."

But I bid farewell to my new found friends and a place
called El Capitan,
The fairest faces I ever saw was in this proud and happy
band.
I climbed into my saddle and started out for home;
I made up my mind right there and then I never more
would roam.

I am a Mor-mon cow-boy, ___ U - tah is my
home, Tuc - son, Ar - i - zo - na, is the
first place I did roam, And then in - to El
Cap - i - tan, a place you all know well, To de -
scribe that brush-y coun-try, no mor-tal tongue can tell.

Mustang Grey

This ancient song from Texas has been in print for years, but I only learned its haunting melody when Tom Carter took a couple of versions from Fife's and Lingenfeld's and Dwyer's books and stuck them together with a bit of his own creative glue.

There was a noble ranger,
His name was Mustang Grey,
He left his home when but a youth,
Went rangin' far away.

Refrain:

But he'll go no more a rangin',
The savage to afright,
He has heard his last war whoop
And fought his last fight.

He ne'er would sleep within a tent,
No comfort would he know,
But like a brave old Texian,
A rangin' he would go.

When Texas was invaded
By a mighty tyrant foe,
He mounted on his war horse
And rangin' he did go.

Refrain

Once he was taken prisoner,
Bound in chains along the way,
He wore the yoke of bondage
Through the streets of Monterey.

A señorita loved him
And followed by his side,

She set him free and gave to him
Her father's steed to ride.

God bless the señorita,
The belle of Monterey,
She opened wide the prison doors
And let him ride away.

Refrain

And when this veteran's life was spent,
It was his last command
To bury him on Texas soil
On the banks of the Rio Grande.

And there the lonely traveller,
When passing by his grave,
Can shed a fond and farewell tear
To the bravest of the brave.

Refrain

There was a no-ble ran-ger, _ His name was Mus-tang
Grey, He left his home when but a youth, Went
rang-in' far a-way. But he'll go no more a
rang-in', The sav-age to a-fright, He has
heard _ his last war whoop And fought _ his last fight.

The Night Herding Song

This is an old song probably written by Harry Stephens of Denison, Texas. The version I like is a smoother, more melancholy version learned from the Girls of the Golden West.

Refrain (also repeat after each verse):

Hi-O-Hi-O-Hi-O
Hi-O-Hi-O-Hi-O

Oh slow up, dogies, quit your roamin' 'round,
You've wandered and trampled all over the ground;
Go graze along, dogies, and feed kinda slow
And don't be forever on the go.
Move slow, dogies, move slow.

Oh say, little dogies, when you goin' to lay down,
Quit this forever siftin' around?
My limbs are weary, my seat is sore,
Oh lay down, dogies, like you've laid before,
Lay down, dogies, lay down.

O lay still, dogies, since you have laid down,
Stretch your way out on the big open ground;
Snore loud, little dogies, and drown the wild sound;
They'll all go 'way when the day rolls 'round.
Lay still, dogies, lay still.

Nighttime In Nevada

Each state has its official state song, and there is usually an unofficial state folk song. This is Nevada's. It came my way through Larry Schutte, a buckaroo from Tuscarora, Nevada, who used to hear the Sons of the Pioneers sing it at rural Nevada Casinos.

When it's nighttime in Nevada I'm dreamin'
Of the old days on the desert and you.
I miss you when the campfires are gleamin',
And I wonder if you miss me too.
I can see the Great Divide and the trails we used to ride,
The only bit of heaven I knew.
When it's nighttime in Nevada I'm dreamin'
Of the old days on the desert and you.

Refrain:

I've been driftin' since we've roamed the ranges,
Up to roamin' when you went away,
With the love for you that never changes,
I hope that we will meet again some day.
Repeat the verse.

Old Alberta Plains
Wilf Carter

This Canadian song, written by an Alberta cowboy early in his recording career, tells of love of place, a common theme in cowboy songs of the '30s and '40s. Better known as Montana Slim, the author is one of the great cowboy yodelers.

There's a spot that is dear to the heart of old cowboys
Who once rode broncos, darn hard to tame,
A-hittin' the saddle at the first streak of daylight,
Singin' a song of old Alberta plains.

Refrain:

Oh carry me back to the plains of Alberta,
I long to go back to the wide rolling range,
On a bright sunny hillside I'd sit there a dreamin',
Those good old days on old Alberta plains.

Refrain

The low of the cattle, the flamin' sun settin',
Brandin' the strays, that ain't none to blame,
Up rose the chuck wagon and the old cook
    complainin',
It's all in the life on old Alberta range.

Refrain

I've ridden the ranges they call dear old Texas,
Crossed to Montana, to me they're the same;
There's no place on earth that I love so sincerely,
To be back again on old Alberta plains.

Refrain

Pale moon is ridin' high up in the heaven,
Feelin' so lonely, heart full of pain,
If I only could swing once more in the saddle,
As I did years ago on old Alberta plains.

Refrain

The Old Chisolm Trail

This is a wonderful but simple song which lends itself to making up your own verses. My group sings some of the more standard couplets, owing to our credo to attain a high standard of standardness in our music. We learned it from Haywire "Mac" McClintock.

With a ten-dollar horse and a forty-dollar saddle,
I'm goin' to punchin' them long-horned cattle.

Refrain (after each couplet):
Come a ti-yi-yippi-yippi-aye-yippi-aye,
Come a ti-yi-yippi-yippi-aye.

It's up in the morning, before daylight,
And before I sleep the moon shines bright.

It's cloudy in the west, and it looks like rain,
And my danged old slicker's in the wagon again.

With feet in the stirrup, and my hand on the horn,
I'm the best dang cowboy ever was born,

I went to the boss, for to draw my roll,
He had it figured nine dollars in the hole.

So I sold my horse, and I sold my saddle,
And I bid farewell to them long-horned cattle.

With a ten - dol - lar horse and a

for - ty dol - lar sad - dle, I'm goin' to punch-in' them

Refrain

long-horned cat - tle. Come a ti - yi - yi - pi - yi - pi -

aye - yi - pi - aye, Come a ti - yi - yi - pi - yi - pi - aye.

Old Paint Waltz

A good percentage of cowboy songs are in waltz time. This song has the tradition of being the last waltz at cowboy dances. This ancient version came from the fiddling and singing of Jess Morris of Dalhart, Texas. Though this melody is somewhat different than standard, with a little fiddling around, the words fit with the more familiar melody.

Farewell fair ladies, I'm leavin' Cheyenne,
Farewell fair ladies, I'm leavin' Cheyenne,
Goodbye my little Dony, my pony won't stand.

Refrain (after each verse):

Old Paint, old Paint, I'm leavin' Cheyenne,
Goodbye old Paint, I'm leavin' Cheyenne,
Old Paint's a good pony, she paces when she can.

In the middle of the ocean there grows a green tree,
And I'll never prove false to the girl that loves me.

Oh spread down your blanket on the green grassy
    ground,
And the horse and cattle are a-grazin' all around.

Last time I saw her it was late in the fall,
She was ridin' old Paint, a-leadin' old Ball.

Old Paint had a colt down on the Rio Grande,
And the colt couldn't pace and they named it Cheyenne.

My feet's in my stirrup, my bridle's in my hand,
Goodbye my little Dony, my pony won't stand.

Farewell fair ladies, I'm leavin' Cheyenne,
Farewell fair ladies, I'm leavin' Cheyenne,
Goodbye my little Dony, my pony won't stand.

Fare - well fair _ la-dies, I'm lea-vin' Chey - enne, _ Fare -

well fair _ la - dies, I'm lea-vin' Chey - enne, Good -

bye my lit - tle Do - ny, my po - ny won't stand.

Refrain

Old Paint, Old Paint, I'm lea-vin' Chey - enne, Good -

bye Old Paint, I'm lea - vin' Chey - enne, _ Old

Paint's a good po - ny, she pa-ces when she can.

Old-Time Trapper

This song, as well as "Dryland Farmers," came to me through Ward Atwood. He said some friends got snowed in for a winter and made this up on a long winter's night in a Montana cabin.

Oh, I am an old-time trapper and I've roamed all o'er
    the streams
Lived on corn bread, bacon, and beans.
In that glorious valley where the river Judith flows
I caught the fine fur bear where that diamond willow
    grows.

Now we'll trap no more on the Judith, the muddy
    Musselshell
For I'm goin' up into Canada where I'll round 'em in a
    corral.

And when I've gone a few short years, I will begin to
    save
And bring it back to old Montana to the place I love so
    well,
To the little town of Two Dot on the banks of the
    muddy Musselshell.

Oh, I am an old-time trapper and I've roamed all o'er the streams Lived on corn bread bacon and beans. In that glorious valley where the river Judith flows I caught that fine fur bear where the diamond willow grows. Now we'll trap no more on the Judith, nor the muddy Mussel-shell For I'm goin' up into Canada where I'll round 'em in a corral. And when I've gone a few short years, I will begin to save And bring it back to Old Montana to the place I love so well, To the little town of Two Dot on the banks of the muddy Mussel-shell.

Powder River, Let 'Er Buck

Powder River Jack Lee, a performer in early wild west shows, probably wrote this one, though his claims to authorship of certain other poems throws a shadow on his credibility—who knows. Anyway, it's a great song full of imagery and a lexicon of cowboy lingo.

Powder River, let 'er buck,
A surgin' mass of cattle,
Roundup wagons full of chuck,
Horns and hoofs a-rattle.
Steers and dogies, beefs and broncs,
Heavin' flanks a-quiver,
Hear the wranglers yip "Whoopee,
Hooray for Powder River."

Clouds of dust and ropes a-whirl
Snubbin' broncs a-standin',
Bellerin' mavericks holdin' down,
Every outfit brandin'.
Deep the mud and cold the rain,
Loud the claps of thunder,
Slickers nigh for buckaroos
And waddies crawlin' under.

(Shout)
Powder River, let 'er buck,
Whoa, you ornery raw-boned, crop-eared, loco, son of
    Satan, whoa.

Loud the steers and heifers bawl,
And dogies all a-roamin',
Strays set out for stompin' grounds
And headin' for Wyoming.
Bridles off for feedin' grounds,
Horns and hoofs a-rattle,

One eye open, half asleep,
A-herdin' ornery cattle.

Old Red Smith, the wagon cook,
Bakin' beans and liver,
They're wild and they don't care a cuss,
The boys from Powder River.
Cookie yells through pots and pans,
"C'mon you ornery guzzards,
Come and git 'er or out she goes,
Or I'll feed 'er to the buzzards."

(Shout)
Come and git 'er you ornery sons of mavericks or I'll
    feed 'er to the hungry coyotes. Heist your legs,
    cowboys.

Herders left and herders right,
Broncs and cuttin' horses,
Sougans under starry skies,
Wagons for the bosses.
Old chinook, it's changin' west,
Angry bulls a-boomin',
Straight above the feedin' grounds,
Rocky Mountains loomin'.

Floppin' hats and shaggy chaps,
Dogies all a-shiver,
"Top screws out" and "spool your beds,"
And "home for Powder River."
Circlin' riders singin' low,
Zoomin' o'er the prairies;
Pens a-buldge and hear them shout,
"We're goin' to see our Marys."

(Shout)
Powder River full of dust and flat fish, cross 'er
    anywhere.

Thunderin' hoofs across the range,
Sunburned hides and faces,
Twisters spinnin' east and west,
And cowboys runnin' races.
"Scratch your broncs, you ridin' fools,"
A big whoopee they give her,
"We're wild and woolly, full of fleas,
And bound for Powder River."

(Shout)
She's one mile wide, an inch deep, and she rolls uphill
    from Texas.

Pow-der Ri-ver, let 'er buck, A surg-in' mass of cat-tle,

Round-up wa-gons full of chuck, Horns and hoofs a - rat-tle.

Steers and do-gies, beefs and broncs, Heav-in' flanks a - qui-ver,

Hear the wrang-lers yip "Whoop-ee, Hoo-ray for Pow-der Ri-ver."

Clouds of dust and ropes a-whirl, Snub-bin' broncs a - stan-din',

Bell-er-in' mave-ricks hol-din' down, _ Ev-ery out-fit brand-in'.

Deep the mud and cold the rain, Loud the claps of thun-der,

Slick-ers nigh for buck-a-roos, And wad-dies crawl-in' un-der.

Railroading On The Great Divide
The Carter Family

T his version is sung by **Skip Gorman.**

Nineteen and sixteen when I started to roam
Out in the West, no money, no home,
I just drifted along with the tide,
I landed on the Great Divide.

Refrain:

Railroading on the Great Divide,
Nothing around me but the Rockies and the sky,
There you will find me as the years roll by
Railroading on the Great Divide.

As I looked out across the field,
Number Three's coming, the fastest on wheels;
Through old Laramie she glides with pride
And she rolls across the Great Divide.

Refrain

Ask any old-timer from old Cheyenne,
Railroading in Montana's the best in the land—
The long steel rails and the short cross ties,
I landed on the Great Divide.

Refrain

Red River Valley

Sentimentality has fallen into disfavor in modern artistic
expression. It's hard to appreciate Victorian art without
it. Cowboy art is at its sentimental best in this Canadian
classic.

From this valley they say you are going,
I shall miss your sweet face and bright smile.
For they say you are taking the sunshine
That has brightened my pathway awhile.

Refrain (after each verse):

Come and sit by my side if you love me.
Do not hasten to bid me adieu,
For remember the Red River Valley
And the cowboy who loved you so true.

There never could be such a longing
In the heart of a poor cowboy's breast,
As dwells in this heart you are breaking
While I wait in my home in the West.

Do you think of this valley you're leaving,
Oh, how lonely and dreary it will be?
Do you think of the kind hearts you're grieving,
And the pain you are causing to me?

From this valley they say you are going
I will miss your bright eyes and sweet smile,
For they say you are weary and tired
And must find a new range for a while.

From this val – ley they say you are go – ing, ____ ____ I shall miss your sweet face and bright smile. ____ For they say you are tak – ing the sun – shine ____ That has bright – ened my path for a – while. ____

Red Whiskey

This is one of the great staples of old-time fiddling. Sometimes called "Rye Whiskey" or "Drunken Hiccups," this one has been fiddled all over the country. It captures the tenuous relationship between fiddle music and inebriation. Our words come from Dick Duval.

I've rambled, I've trampled, I've rambled around.
I'm going back to cow country, To cow country I'm
 bound.

I ride wild horses while rambling around.
I can ride the wildest bronco that's ever been found.

Refrain:

"Red whiskey, red whiskey, red whiskey," I cry.
If I don't get red whiskey I surely will die.

Jack o' diamonds, Jack o' diamonds, I know you of old,
You robbed my poor pockets of silver and gold.

If the ocean was whiskey, and I was a duck,
I'd dive to the bottom for one sweet cup.

But the ocean ain't whiskey, and I ain't no duck,
So play the Jack o'diamonds and go get drunk.

Refrain

O Molly, O Molly, I've told you before,
Go make me a pallet, I'll sleep on your floor.

It's beefsteak when I'm hungry, Corn whiskey when
 I'm dry,
Pretty girls when I'm lonesome, Sweet
 heaven when I die.

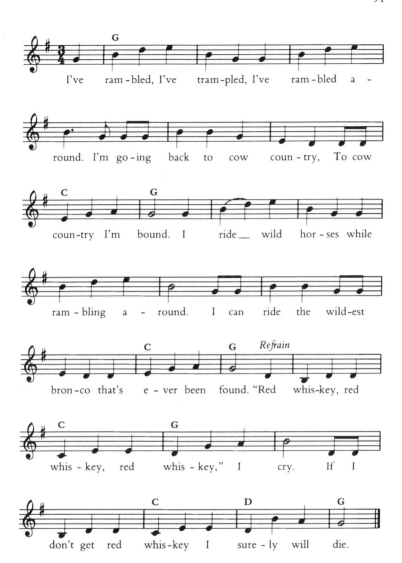

The Roving Cowboy

This version comes through old-timer Frank Jenkins, who sang and played it on the fiddle—which takes rare dexterity.

Come all you roving cowboys, bound down this lonely
  land.
I'll tell to you a story, while you around me stand.
I'm going to quit this wild West, its big and stormy
  plain,
For I think I'm going to leave you to never return again.

So sweetheart, my dear sweetheart, your faithful's
  bound to roam,
I left my dear old father, my country and home.
I left my dear old mother so weak and alone
To be a roving cowboy and live and travel alone.

I left my home in Texas with many a parting tear,
My father's voice was saying, "my boy, my boy, I fear,
May God protect and guide you and leave you not alone,
And bring this roving cowboy back to his native home."

This maiden fair and lovely sat closely by my side.
That night she promised faithful that she would be my
  bride.
I kissed away her flowing tears, that dimmed her fair
  blue eyes.
I never forgot my darling girl, I'll love her till I die.

I tried to face the barren plains, I know the trails well.
I crossed the Rocky Mountain, where many a brave
  boy fell.
I've seen the far distant country, where the Indians
  roam so wild.
I'll never forget my dear old home or mother's sweetest
  smile.

Come all___ you rov-ing cow-boys, ___ bound down this lone-ly land. ___ I'll tell to you a stor-y, while you a-round me stand. I'm goin' to quit this wild West, its big and storm-y plain, For I think I'm going to leave you _ to ne-ver re-turn a – gain.

The Strawberry Roan
Curley Fletcher

Fletcher wrote this one at the big rodeo in Cheyenne in 1914. It has become one of the great classics in cowboy poetry and music.

I was hangin' 'round town just spendin' my time,
Out of a job, not makin' a dime,
When a stranger steps up, says he, "I suppose
That you're a bronc fighter by the looks of your
    clothes."
"Well, you guesses me right, I'm a good one," I claim.
"Do you happen to have any bad ones to tame?"
He said, "I've got one, a bad one to buck,
    And at throwin' good riders he's had lots of luck."

He says that this pony ain't never been rode,
The man that gets on him is bound to get throwed.
Well, I gets all excited and asks what he pays
If I ride this old cayuse a couple of days.
He offers me ten. Says I, "I'm your man,
For the bronc never lived or ever drew breath
That I couldn't ride till he starved plumb to death."

He says, "Get your saddle, I'll give you a chance."
We hops in the buckboard and rides to his ranch.
I stays until morning, and right after chuck
I goes out to see how this outlaw can buck.
Down in the horse corral, standing alone,
Is this caballo, a strawberry roan.

I got the blind on him with a terrible fight,
Cinched on the saddle and girded it tight;
Then I steps up on him and pulled down the blind
And sat there in the saddle to see him unwind.

He bowed his old neck and I'll say he unwound,
He seemed to quit living down there on the ground;
He went up to the east and came down to the west
With me in the saddle, a-doing my best.

He sure was frog-walkin', I heaved a big sigh,
He only lacked wings for to be on the fly;
He turned his old belly right up to the sun,
For he was a sun-fishin' son of a gun.

He was the worst bronco I've seen on the range,
He could turn on a nickel and leave you some change.
While he was buckin' he squalled like a shoat,
I tell you that outlaw, he sure got my goat.

I tell all the people that pony could step
And I was still on him a-buildin' a rep;
He came down on all fours and turned up his side,
I don't see how he kept from losing his hide.

I lost my stirrup, I lost my hat,
I was pullin' at leather as blind as a bat;
With a phenomenal jump he made a high dive
And set me a-winding up there through the sky.

I turned forty flips and came down to the earth
And sit there a-cussing the day of his birth.
I know there's some ponies that I cannot ride,
Some of them living, they haven't all died—

But I bet all my money there's no man alive
That can ride Old Strawberry when he makes that high
    dive.

I was hang-in' 'round town _ just spend-in' my time,

Out of a job, _ not mak-in' a dime, When a

strang-er steps up, says he, "I sup-pose that

you're a bronc fight-er by the look of your _ clothes." "Well you

guess-es me right, I'm a good one," I claim. "Do you

hap-pen to have an-y bad ones to tame?" He

said, "I've got one, a bad one to buck, and at

throw-in' good ri-ders he's had lots of _ luck."

Texas Rangers

This one was sung by Sloan Matthews of Alpine, Texas, for John Lomax in 1942. It is truly a classic.

Come all ye Texas Rangers wherever you may be,
I'll tell you of some troubles that happened unto me.
My name is nothin' extry and that I will not tell,
And here's to all you rangers, I'm sure I wish you well.

'Twas at the age of seventeen I joined the jolly band.
We marched from San Antonio down to the Rio
    Grande.
Our captain he informed us, Perhaps he thought it
    right,
"Before we reach the station, boys, you'll surely have
    to fight."

And when the bugles sounded, our captain gave
    command.
"To arms, to arms," he shouted, "and by your horses
    stand."
I saw the smoke ascending, it seemed to reach the sky,
And then the thought it struck me, my time had come
    to die.

I saw the Indians coming, I heard them give a yell.
My feelings at that moment no tongue can ever tell.
I saw their glittering lances, their arrows round me
    flew,
And all my strength it left me, and all my courage, too.

We fought for nine hours fully before the strife was
   o'er.
The like of dead and wounded I never saw before.
And when the sun had risen and the Indians they had
   fled
We loaded up our rifles and counted up our dead.

All of us were wounded, our noble captain slain.
The sun was shining sadly across the bloody plain.
Sixteen as brave a rangers as ever roamed the West
Were buried by their comrades with arrows in their
   breast.

And now my song is ended, I guess I sung enough.
The life of any ranger, you see, is very tough.
And if you have a mother that don't want you to roam,
I advise you, by experience, you'd better stay at home.

Come all ye Tex-as Rang-ers wher - ev - er you may be,

I'll _ tell you of some troub-les that hap-pened un-to me.

Trail To Mexico

This melody is one that grows on you. Sing it daily for a year or two and you will find out. We learned this from Slim Critchlow.

I made up my mind to change my ways
And quit my crowd that was so gay,
To leave my native home for a while
And travel out West for many a mile.

It was in the year of eighty-three
That A. J. Stinson done hired me.
He said, "Young fellow I want you to go
And follow my herd to Mexico."

Well it was early in the year
That I went on the trail to drive them steers.
I stood my guard in the sleet and the snow
While on the trail to Mexico.

Well it was a long and lonesome go
As the herd rolled on to Mexico,
With laughter light and the cowboy's song,
To Mexico we rolled along.

When we arrived in Mexico
I wanted to see my love, but I couldn't go,
So I wrote a letter, a letter to my dear,
But not one word from her did I hear.

When I got back to my once-loved home
I called for my darling I thought my own.
They said she'd married a richer life,
Therefore, wild cowboy, you can seek another wife.

Oh the girl, she's married, I do adore,
I cannot stay at home anymore,
I'll make my way to some foreign land
Or I'll go back to that cowboy band.

Oh buddy, oh buddy, please don't leave home,
Please don't be in a hurry to roam;
There's plenty of girls more true than I,
Oh don't go west where the bullets fly.

It's curse your gold and your silver too.
God pity a girl that don't prove true.
I'll go out West where the bullets fly
And I'll follow the cow trail until I die.

I'll take my bridle in my hand
And I'll go join that cowboy band.
I'll bid farewell to the Alamo
And head my horse to Mexico.

Utah Carol

This is sometimes sung as Utah Carl, but if you are from Utah it is not unusual to meet men named Carol, Shirley, Lynn, or Marion. I learned this song from my old buddy Skip Gorman, who learned it from Carl Sprague.

Kind friends, you may ask me what makes me sad and
   still
And why my brow is darkened like the clouds upon the
   hill;
Reign in your pony closer and I'll tell you a tale
Of Utah Carol, my partner, and his last ride on the
   trail.

We rode the range together and we rode it side by side;
I loved him like a brother and I wept when Utah died;
We were rounding up one morning and our work was
   almost done,
When on one side they started on a mad and fearful run.

The boss man's little daughter was holding on that side,
She waved a bright red blanket, they charged with
   maddened fear;
Little Varo, seeing the danger, knew she would have to
   ride;
A leaning in the saddle she flung the blanket in the air.

And leaning she lost her balance, fell in front of that
   wild tide;
Utah then wildly shouted, "Lay still, Varo," he cried.
His only hope was to raise her and catch her at full speed
As oft times he'd been known to catch a trail rope off his
   steed.

But the cinches of his saddle had not been felt before,
And the back cinch snapped asunder and he fell beside
    Varo;
He picked up the red blanket and he waved it o'er his
    head,
Then he started across the prairie, "Lay still, Varo," he
    said.

Well he got the stampede turned and he saved Varo, his
    friend,
Then he turned to face the cattle and meet his fatal end.
And when we broke the circle where Utah's body lay
With many a bruise and wound, his good life ebbed
    away.

Utah Trail
Bob Palmer

This pop song published in 1928 has become a folk favorite in the Utah country.

You ask me where I'm goin' so early in the dawn.
I'm just a trav'ler roving, just a-roamin' on.
I've looked this old world over, many times have
    searched in vain
For a spot that seems like heaven to me and I long to be
    again.

I'm goin' to hide away out beside the Utah trail.
Moonlight as bright as day far out on that Utah trail.
There's where I'll settle down in peace where all is still,
In a little hut just built for two tucked away in the heart
    of the hills.

There 'neath the skies of blue in the golden
    summertime,
Out where all friends are true and all nature is in rhyme,
Someone is waiting with a love that never fails,
Waiting patiently to welcome me far out on that Utah
    trail.

rhyme, Some - one is wait - ing with a love that ne - ver fails___ Wait-ing pa-tient - ly to wel-come me far out on that U - tah trail.

We Left Our Homes In Utah
John Averett and Dave Cook

This song reflects the personal experience of the authors, who were called to guard the Colorado River along the Arizona Strip against Indian attacks. We learned it from John Averett's niece, Della Turner. Though many songs in this book are best sung unaccompanied, this one defies guitar chords, which all but ruin its haunting melody.

We left our homes in Utah, it seemed so very hard,
To go the Colorado and there keep up our guard,
Where the wind it blew so hard and the sand it was so
    thick,
We had to clean our eyes out with a spade and pick.

We traveled on a few days until we got to Lees'
When a cow jumped over our wagon tongue and broke
    our whipple tree.
We wrapped it up with a stay chain and tied it with a
    string,
And worked it on to Kanab and got it fixed again.

We stayed all night at this place, we had a little ball.
The music it was good, but the house it was so small.
Then when we all got in it we couldn't turn around,
So we went out in the door yard and danced upon the
    ground.

We traveled on to Windsors' we had another ball;
The house it was large enough to accommodate us all.
The girls they were so pretty and they danced so very gay;
We danced till we got tired and then we went away.

We traveled on to Johnsons' our orders to receive,
And here it was hot as hell without a bit o' breeze,
And when the wind it did come it all came in a flirt,
And golly it was hot enough to almost burn your shirt.

And now we're in the river and the rocks they are so high,
You can't see out but one place and that's up to the sky.
The river is so muddy and it smells just like the breeze,
That comes from the little house that stands among the trees.

Oh, our tea is full of sand and our bread is full of grit.
The wind it blows all over us whenever it sees fit.
So talk about your gritty men, I think we'll take the prize,
For we're sanded in and outside and all around the eyes.

a capella

We left our homes in U - tah, it seemed so ver - y hard, — To go the Col - o - ra - do and there keep up our guard, — Where the wind it blew so hard and the sand it was so thick, — We — had to clean our eyes out with a spade and pick.

Western Pioneer

Thﬁs is one of the earliest cowboy songs I know of, made
up even before cowboys had any romantic appeal. The
melody was recovered through a snipit of a verse sung into a
tape recorder by Ezra Barhight. After the one verse he stub-
bornly states, "And I won't sing any more till I have supper."

Come, give me your attention and see the right and
    wrong,
It is a simple story and it won't detain you long;
I'll try to tell the reason why we are bound to roam,
And why we are so friendless and never have a home.

My home is in the saddle, upon a pony's back,
I am a roving cowboy and find the hostile track;
They say I am a sure shot, and danger I never knew;
But I often heard a story which I'll relate to you.

In eighteen hundred and sixty-three a little emigrant
    band
Was massacred by Indians, bound West by overland;
They scalped our noble soldiers, and the emigrants had
    to die,
And the only living captives were two small girls and I.

We were rescued from the Indians by a brave and noble
    man,
Who trailed the thieving Indians and fought them hand
    to hand;
He was noted for his bravery while on an enemy's
    track;
He had a noble history, his name is Texas Jack.

Old Jack could tell a story, if he was only here,
Of the trouble and the hardships of the Western
    pioneer;

He would tell you how our fathers and mothers lost
their lives,
And how our aged parents were scalped before our
eyes.

I am a roving cowboy, I've worked upon the trail,
I've shot the shaggy buffalo and heard the coyote's wail;
I have slept upon my saddle, all covered by the moon;
I expect to keep it up, dear friends, until I meet my
doom.

I am a roving cowboy, my saddle is my home,
And I'll always be a cowboy, no difference where I
roam;
And like our noble heroes my help I'll volunteer,
And try to be of service to the Western pioneer.

When The Work's All Done This Fall
D. J. O'Malley

O'Malley wrote this in 1886 for the Montana Stock Grower's Journal. It became a popular song with cowboys. In 1924 Carl Sprague recorded it for Victor and it sold nearly a million copies.

A group of jolly cowboys, discussing plans at ease,
Says one, "I'll tell you something if you will listen
   please.
I am an old cowpuncher, and here I'm dressed in rags.
I used to be a tough one and go on great big jags.

"But I have got a home boys, and a good one you all
   know,
Although I haven't seen it since long, long ago.
I'm going back to Dixie once more to see them all,
I'm going to see my mother when the work's all done
   this fall.

"When I left my home, boys, my mother for me cried,
She begged me not to go, boys, for me she would have
   died.
My mother's heart is breaking, breaking for me that's
   all,
And with God's help I'll see her when the work's all
   done this fall."

That very night this cowboy went out to stand his
   guard,
The night was dark and cloudy and storming very hard.
The cattle all got frightened, and rushed in wild
   stampede,
The cowboy tried to head them, while riding at full
   speed.

While riding in the darkness, so loudly did he shout,
Trying his best to head them and turn the herd about.
His saddle horse did stumble and on him it did fall,
The boy won't see his mother when the work's all done
    this fall.

His body was so mangled, the boys all thought him
    dead.
They picked him up so gently and laid him on a bed;
He opened wide his blue eyes, and looking all around,
He motioned to his comrades to sit near on the ground.

"Boys, send mother my wages, the wages I have
    earned,
For I am so afraid boys, the last steer I have turned.
I'm going to a new range, I hear my Master's call,
And I'll not see my mother when the work's all done
    this fall.

"Fred, you take my saddle, George, you take my bed;
Bill, you take my pistol after I am dead.
Then please think of me kindly when you look upon
    them all,
For I'll not see my mother when the work's all done this
    fall."

Poor Charlie was buried at sunrise, no tombstone at his
    head,
Nothing but a little slab, and this is what it said:
"Charlie died at daybreak, He died from a fall.
And he'll not see his mother when the work's all done
    this fall."

113

A group of jol-ly cow-boys, dis-cuss-ing plans at ease, Says one, "I'll tell you some-thing if you will lis-ten please. I am an old cow-punch-er, and here I'm dressed in rags. I used to be a tough one __ and go on great big jags."

Whoopee-ti-yi-o Git Along Little Dogies

Every cowboy has a distinct whistle, call, or shout for driving cattle. Never have I heard anyone drive a cow with a whoopee-ti-yi-o. That doesn't mean it isn't a good old song though. This version is from Texas's Cartwright Brothers.

As I was out walking one morning for pleasure
I spied a cowpuncher a–ridin' along.
His hat was pushed back and his spurs were a–jinglin'
And as he approached he was singing this song.

Refrain (after each verse)

Whoop–ee–ti–yi–o get along little dogies,
It's your misfortune and none of my own.
Whoop–ee–ti–yi–o get along little dogies,
You know Wyoming will be your new home.

It's early in the springtime we round up the dogies;
We rope 'em and brand 'em and bob off their tails,
Round up the horses, load up the chuck wagons,
And drive them dogies out on the trail.

It's whoopin' and a–yellin' and drivin' those dogies,
O how I do wish they would go on.
It's whoopin' and yellin' and drivin' those dogies,
You know Wyoming will be their new home.

If I ever marry it'll be to a widow
With fourteen children, not one of my own;
If I every marry it'll be to a widow
With a great big ranch and a ten-story home.

As I was out walk-ing one morn-ing for

plea-sure I spied a cow-punch-er a - rid - in' a -

long. His hat was pushed back and his spurs were a -

jing-lin' And as he ap - proached he was sing-ing this

Refrain

song. _____ Whoop-ee — ti — yi — o get a -

long lit-tle do-gies, It's your mis - for-tune and

none of my own. Whoop-ee — ti — yi — o get a -

long lit - tle do - gies, You know Wy -

o - ming will be your new home.

Wyoming Home

This one is a longtime favorite which comes from the Dixon Brothers. Unlike "Utah Trail" and "Nightime in Nevada," I have never sung this in Wyoming to anyone who has heard it before.

There's a place in Wyoming I'm longing to be,
Where the air is so pure and the wind blows free,
Where the cowboys gather 'round the campfire so
     bright,
To yodel and sing in the lone starry night.

1st Refrain:

Roll on little dogies, roll on, roll on,
Roll on little dogies, roll on.

Night after night I sit all alone,
Watching the stars and the pale silvery moon;
My fancy nearby, my pinto I see,
Back in Wyoming I'm longing to be.

2nd Refrain:

Oh, my Wyoming home, my dear old Wyoming
     home,
I'll jump in my saddle and away I will ride
Over the hills and across the Divide,
Back to my Wyoming home.

There's a home in Wyoming I left long ago,
Left me with memories that I cherish so;
A grey-haired mother and a little red shack,
Songs of the prairie are calling me back.

1st Refrain`

I'm leaving today for a Wyoming town
To see all my friends and the cowboys around.
No one knows how glad I will be
When I can find mother a-waiting for me.

2nd Refrain

dear old Wy - o - ming home, _____ I'll jump in my sad - dle and a - way I will ride O - ver the hills and a - cross the Di - vide, Back to my Wy - o - ming home. _____

Further Reading and Listening

This book and cassette contain only a few of a vast repertoire of cowboy songs. Sources for some others of my favorites are listed below.

Books

Fife, Austin, and Fife, Alta. *Cowboy and Western Songs, A Comprehensive Anthology.* New York: Clarkson S. Potter, Bramhall Press, 1969.

Lee, Katie. *Ten Thousand God Damned Cattle.* Flagstaff: Northland Press, 1976.

Lingenfelter, Richard E., and Dwyer, Richard A. *Songs of the American West.* Berkeley and Los Angeles: University of California Press, 1968.

Lomax, John, Lomax, Alan. *Cowboy Songs and Other Frontier Ballads.* New York: MacMillan Books, 1986.

Ohrlin, Glenn. *The Hell-bound Train: A Cowboy Songbook.* Urbana: University of Illinois Press, 1973.

Thorpe, N. Howard "Jack." *Songs of the Cowboys.* New York: Bramhall House, 1966. Originally published in 1908 but republished here with notes by the Fifes.

Tinsley, Jim Bob. *He Was Singing This Song.* Orlando: University of Florida Press, 1981.

White, John I. *Git Along Little Dogies.* Urbana: University of Illinois Press, 1975.

Recordings

Authentic Cowboys and Their Western Folksongs. Fred Hoeptner, ed. RCA Vintage Series, LPV-552.

Back in the Saddle Again. Charlie Seemann, ed. New World Records, NW 324–315.

Carl Sprague: The First Popular Singing Cowboy. Folk Variety Records, FV 12001.

Harry Jackson: The Cowboy, His Songs, Ballads, and Talk. Harry Jackson. Folkways, FH 5723.

Cowboy Songs, Vols. 1 and 2. Arizona Friends of Folklore, AFF 33-1 and 2.

Cowboy Songs, Ballads, and Cattle Calls from Texas. Duncan Emrich, ed. Library of Congress, R53-318 rev.

Cowboy Songs: "The Crooked Trail to Holbrook." Slim Critchlow. Arhoolie Records, 5007.

Deseret String Band. Schanachie Records, 79041.

The Girls of the Golden West. Sonyatone Records, STR-202.

Harry K. McClintock: "Haywire Mac", Folkways Records, FD 5272.

Fences, Barbed Wire, and Walls. Horse Sense, Kicking Mule

Records, 338.

New Beehive Songsters, Vols. 1 and 2. University of Utah Press, 0-87480-175-3.

The Plains of Alberta: A Collection of Early Cowboy Songs. Historical Records, HLP 8007.

Powder River. Skip Gorman and Ron Kane. Folk Legacy Records, FSI 76.

Singin' Sam Agins. Haywire, ARA 6419.

Songs of the West. George Hocutt, ed. Glendale Records, GL6020.

The Texas Cowboy. Jules Verne Allen. Folk Variety Records, FV 12502.

Trail to Mexico. Skip Gorman. Folk Legacy Records.

When I Was a Cowboy: Classic Recordings of the 1920's. Richard Nevins, ed. Morning Star Records, 45008.

When the Work's All Done This Fall: Songs, Stories, and Poems from Montana Cattle Camps and Cow Trails. Mike Korn, ed. Montana Folklife Project.

The Wild Buckaroo. Glenn Ohrlin. Rounder Records, 0158. Ohrlin has recorded other L.P.s for Philo Records.

Book and Recording Distributors

Cowboy Poetry Gathering
Box 888
Elko, NV 89801

Down Home Records
10341 San Pablo Ave.
El Cerrito, CA 94530

Shanachie Records
Dalebrook Park
Hohokus, NJ 07423

County Sales
Box 191
Floyd, VA 24091

Round-up Records
P.O. Box 154
North Cambridge, MA 02140